FLEET MANAGEMENT 101

A BLUEPRINT FOR OPERATIONAL SUCCESS

2023

DOBBS MEDIA

Table of Contents

Introduction

In today's fast-paced world, where the movement of goods, services, and people forms the backbone of the global economy, effective fleet management has emerged as a pivotal component to ensure business efficacy, sustainability, and profitability. Fleet management is not merely about managing a group of vehicles. It encompasses a vast array of responsibilities including, but not limited to, optimizing operational costs, ensuring safety, adhering to regulatory compliance, and steering towards environmental responsibility. This guide, "Fleet Management 101: A Blueprint for Operational Success", delves into the nuances of this intricate domain, aiming to equip professionals and enthusiasts with knowledge and best practices.

The Importance of Fleet Management in the Modern World

1. **Economic Impact**: Fleets, ranging from delivery trucks, service vans, to passenger buses and more, play an integral role in the global economy. Effective fleet management ensures

timely delivery of goods and services, directly impacting businesses' bottom lines and the larger economy's health. Mismanagement can lead to significant losses, both financially and in terms of reputation.

2. **Environmental Responsibility**: With growing concerns about environmental degradation and global warming, fleet managers are under increasing pressure to reduce carbon footprints. Modern fleet management involves making sustainable choices, from selecting fuel-efficient vehicles to optimizing routes for minimal emissions.

3. **Safety and Compliance**: Road safety is paramount. Efficient fleet management encompasses driver training, vehicle maintenance, and adherence to safety regulations, ensuring not just the safety of the fleet's drivers, but also that of the public. Additionally, in many regions, non-compliance with vehicular and transport regulations can lead to hefty fines and legal consequences.

4. **Operational Efficiency**: The modern world demands speed and efficiency. Customers expect timely deliveries, and any delay can lead to dissatisfaction and lost business opportunities. Proper fleet management ensures that vehicles are well-maintained, routes are optimized, and operations run seamlessly.

5. **Technological Advancements**: With the advent of technologies such as telematics, AI, and IoT, fleet management has transformed. Embracing these technologies offers unparalleled efficiencies, predictive analytics, and real-time decision-making capabilities.

Overview of the Guide's Contents

"Mastering Fleet Management: A Comprehensive Guide" offers a deep dive into all aspects of fleet management:

- **Foundations**: Begin your journey with an understanding of the basic principles, history, and evolution of fleet management.

- **Vehicle Lifecycle**: Delve into the intricacies of vehicle acquisition, operations, maintenance, and eventual disposal or replacement strategies.

- **Technological Integration**: Explore the world of fleet management software, real-time tracking, and predictive data analytics.

- **Operations and Maintenance**: Understand the nuances of route optimization, driver management, and the importance of regular vehicle upkeep.

- **Safety and Compliance**: Learn about the importance of driver training, safety culture, and the ever-changing regulatory landscape.

- **Sustainability**: Discover the importance of green fleet management, the transition to electric vehicles, and strategies to reduce environmental impact.

- **Future of Fleet Management**: Peek into the future with discussions on autonomous vehicles, AI integration, and the changing dynamics of fleet ownership.

As we navigate through these chapters, you'll gain insights, strategies, and best practices to master the art and science of fleet management in the modern world. Whether you're a seasoned fleet manager, a business owner, or a curious reader, this guide promises to be a valuable resource.

Chapter 1: Foundations of Fleet Management

Definition and Objectives of Fleet Management

Fleet Management can be succinctly defined as the systematic administration and coordination of specific tasks associated with vehicles used by organizations. This management process optimizes costs, risks, and efficiencies while ensuring that the fleet remains operational, safe, and in compliance with relevant regulations. The central objectives of fleet management include:

1. **Operational Efficiency**: Ensuring that the fleet operates at its optimum capacity, resulting in timely service or deliveries, reduced downtime, and maximum utilization of vehicles.

2. **Cost Management**: Minimizing operational and ownership costs through strategic decision-making in areas like maintenance, fuel management, and vehicle acquisition.

3. **Risk Management**: Identifying and mitigating potential risks, ensuring safety standards, and ensuring compliance with regional and global regulations.

4. **Lifespan Optimization**: Prolonging the serviceable life of fleet vehicles through regular maintenance and strategic replacement.

5. **Environmental Responsibility**: Emphasizing sustainable practices, like using fuel-efficient vehicles, adopting cleaner fuels, and implementing efficient route planning to reduce the carbon footprint.

History and Evolution of Fleet Management

The realm of fleet management has not always been as sophisticated as it is today. Its journey can be traced back through the following eras:

1. **Pre-Modern Era (Before the 20th Century)**: This period saw the management of horse-drawn carriages, carts, and wagons. The focus was predominantly on maintaining the health of the

animals, repairing carriages, and ensuring safety on rudimentary road networks.

2. **Early 20th Century**: The advent of motor vehicles marked a significant transition. Organizations started maintaining fleets of cars, trucks, and buses. Initial management strategies revolved around basic maintenance and ensuring vehicles' operational readiness.

3. **Mid to Late 20th Century**: Technological advancements, especially the advent of computers, played a pivotal role. Software solutions began aiding in tracking vehicle maintenance, driver schedules, and rudimentary route optimizations.

4. **Late 20th to Early 21st Century**: GPS and mobile communications transformed fleet management. Real-time tracking, advanced route optimization, and telematics became the new norm. The emphasis also shifted towards sustainability and reducing environmental impact.

5. **Modern Era**: Today, we see the integration of AI, IoT, and big data analytics. The focus is on predictive maintenance, real-time decision-making, autonomous driving capabilities, and a more significant push towards electric and hybrid vehicles.

The Role of Fleet Managers and Their Challenges

Fleet managers are the linchpins of fleet operations. Their roles encompass a broad spectrum of responsibilities:

1. **Operational Oversight**: Ensuring that the fleet is in optimal condition and that operations run seamlessly. This includes scheduling, route planning, and overseeing maintenance.

2. **Financial Management**: Budgeting, cost tracking, and making decisions that ensure financial efficiency.

3. **Compliance and Safety**: Ensuring that the fleet adheres to local and international regulations, while prioritizing safety training and protocols.

4. **Technological Integration**: Adopting and integrating new technologies into the fleet's operations.

5. **Sustainability Initiatives**: Leading the transition to more eco-friendly options, whether through vehicle choices or operational strategies.

Challenges faced by fleet managers are multifaceted:

1. **Evolving Technologies**: Keeping up with rapid technological advancements and ensuring that their benefits are harnessed without incurring excessive costs.

2. **Regulatory Changes**: Navigating a landscape of constantly changing regulations and ensuring compliance.

3. **Economic Pressures**: Balancing financial constraints with the need to maintain an efficient and modern fleet.

4. **Environmental Concerns**: Striving for sustainability while contending with traditional operational practices.

5. **Human Resource Management**: Managing drivers, ensuring their well-being, training, and dealing with shortages or high turnover rates.

In sum, fleet management is a dynamic field that has evolved significantly over the decades. While the core objectives remain largely consistent—efficiency, safety, and cost-effectiveness—the strategies and tools available to achieve these goals have transformed, offering both exciting possibilities and intricate challenges. This chapter serves as a foundational understanding as we delve deeper into the intricacies of modern fleet management in subsequent sections.

Chapter 2: Vehicle Acquisition and Lifecycle Management

Evaluating Needs and Planning Vehicle Acquisition

Before acquiring any vehicles for a fleet, it's imperative to conduct a comprehensive evaluation to determine the organization's needs.

1. **Nature of Operations**: Understand the primary purpose of the fleet. Is it for delivery? Transportation of people? Heavy-duty tasks? Each operation type necessitates different kinds of vehicles.

2. **Volume and Capacity**: Estimate the expected volume of goods or number of people the fleet will handle. This will dictate the size and capacity of the vehicles needed.

3. **Operational Geography**: Consider where the vehicles will operate. Urban settings might require smaller, more maneuverable vehicles,

while long-distance hauls might need larger, durable models.

4. **Budgetary Constraints**: Know your budget. This not only determines the type and number of vehicles you can acquire but also influences the decision between leasing and purchasing.

Leasing vs. Purchasing

Both leasing and purchasing come with their set of advantages and disadvantages.

Leasing

Advantages:

- *Upfront Costs*: Typically, leasing requires less upfront investment compared to purchasing.
- *Flexibility*: Leasing allows for easier fleet upgrades, letting businesses adapt to newer models or technologies.
- *Off-balance-sheet Financing*: Lease obligations can often be kept off the balance sheet, improving financial ratios.

Disadvantages:

- *Long-term Costs*: Over extended periods, leasing may become costlier than owning.
- *Contractual Limitations*: Leases can have restrictions such as mileage limits, wear-and-tear guidelines, and customization restrictions.

Purchasing

Advantages:

- *Asset Ownership*: The vehicle becomes a company asset that can be leveraged or sold.
- *No Usage Restrictions*: No limitations on mileage or wear and tear.
- *Long-term Savings*: Over the lifespan of the vehicle, purchasing might prove to be more economical.

Disadvantages:

- *Depreciation*: Vehicles typically depreciate quickly, which can impact balance sheets.
- *Upfront Capital*: Purchasing requires more immediate capital.

TRAC Leasing

- **Terminal Rental Adjustment Clause (TRAC) Lease**: A TRAC lease is specifically designed for vehicles used in business. It's a type of operating lease where the lessee (business owner) can have an option to purchase the vehicle at the end of the lease term for a predetermined amount, which is usually stipulated in the lease agreement.

Advantages:

- *Flexibility*: Businesses have the option to purchase the vehicle at the end or return it.
- *Lower Monthly Payments*: Since the value of the vehicle at the end of the lease is set in advance (residual value), the monthly payments might be lower compared to other lease structures.
- *Tax Benefits*: Depending on regional regulations, lease payments can often be written off as operational expenses.

Disadvantages:

- *Mileage and Wear Limits*: Like other leases, TRAC leases may have stipulations about the condition and mileage of the vehicle upon return.
- *Potential Additional Costs*: If the market value of the vehicle at the end of the lease term is lower than the predetermined purchase/residual value, the lessee might be responsible for the difference.

Factors Influencing Vehicle Choice

1. **Reliability**: A vehicle's reliability is paramount. Downtime due to breakdowns can be costly. It's essential to consider models known for longevity and fewer mechanical issues.

2. **Fuel Efficiency**: Fuel costs are a significant portion of fleet operational expenses. Selecting fuel-efficient models can lead to substantial savings over the vehicles' lifespan.

3. **Total Cost of Ownership (TCO)**: Beyond the purchase price, consider maintenance costs, fuel consumption, potential resale value, and insurance costs. A vehicle with a lower purchase price might have a higher TCO due to factors like frequent repairs or lower fuel efficiency.

Vehicle Lifecycle: Procurement, Operation, Maintenance, and Disposal

1. **Procurement**:

- *Research and Selection*: Based on the aforementioned factors (reliability, fuel efficiency, and TCO).
- *Negotiation and Financing*: Leveraging bulk buying power or favorable financing terms can lead to significant savings.

2. **Operation**:

- *Route Optimization*: Ensuring vehicles take the most efficient routes, saving on time and fuel.
- *Driver Training*: Proper training ensures the vehicle is used optimally and safely.

3. **Maintenance**:

- *Preventative Maintenance*: Regular checks and services to prevent larger issues.
- *Reactive Maintenance*: Addressing breakdowns or issues as they arise.
- *Record Keeping*: Maintaining comprehensive logs of all maintenance tasks for each vehicle.

4. **Disposal**:

- *Resale*: If the vehicle retains value, it can be sold in the secondary market.
- *Trade-ins*: Older vehicles can sometimes be traded in when acquiring newer ones.
- *Recycling or Scrapping*: In cases where the vehicle is no longer operational and holds minimal value.

Vehicle acquisition and lifecycle management stand at the heart of fleet management. Making informed decisions at each step—evaluating needs, deciding between leasing and purchasing, choosing the right vehicles, and managing them throughout their lifecycle—can be the difference between a fleet that is a financial drain and one that is a key asset driving organizational success.

Chapter 3: Implementing Technology and Data Analysis

Introduction to Fleet Management Software

As the modern world becomes increasingly digital, fleet management has not been left behind. Fleet management software (FMS) offers a unified platform that facilitates various tasks related to fleet operations, from real-time tracking to maintenance scheduling.

1. **Components of FMS**:

- *Vehicle Tracking*: Monitor vehicle locations in real-time.
- *Maintenance Reminders*: Schedule and track routine services and repairs.
- *Fuel Consumption Monitoring*: Keep tabs on fuel usage and costs.
- *Driver Management*: Assess driver behavior, log hours, and track training.

2. **Integration with Other Systems**: Modern FMS can often be integrated with other business systems, like Enterprise Resource Planning (ERP) or Customer Relationship Management (CRM) platforms, providing a holistic view of operations.

Benefits of Telematics and Real-Time Tracking

Telematics, at its core, merges telecommunications and informatics to gather, store, and send information concerning the vehicle back to the organization.

1. **Safety Improvements**: By monitoring driver behaviors such as speeding, hard braking, or rapid acceleration, fleet managers can identify and address risky driving habits.

2. **Operational Efficiency**: Real-time location tracking allows for dynamic route adjustments, redirecting drivers to avoid traffic jams or other obstacles.

3. **Asset Utilization**: By knowing the status and location of every vehicle, managers can ensure optimal asset utilization, reducing downtime or overuse.

4. **Reduced Operational Costs**: By monitoring vehicle health and driving patterns, telematics can help reduce fuel consumption and maintenance costs.

Harnessing Data: Predictive Maintenance, Route Optimization, and Fuel Management

The power of modern FMS lies in its ability to gather vast amounts of data, which, when analyzed correctly, can lead to significant operational improvements.

1. **Predictive Maintenance**:

- *Beyond Reactive Measures*: Instead of waiting for a component to fail, predictive algorithms analyze patterns to predict when parts are likely to wear out or fail, ensuring repairs or replacements before a breakdown occurs.

- *Minimized Downtime*: Predictive maintenance can lead to fewer unexpected breakdowns, reducing vehicle downtime and related costs.

2. **Route Optimization**:

- *Dynamic Adjustments*: Routes can be adjusted in real-time based on traffic, weather, or other unforeseen events.
- *Efficiency and Cost Savings*: By optimizing routes, fleets can reduce mileage, save fuel, and improve delivery times.

3. **Fuel Management**:

- *Monitoring Consumption Patterns*: By understanding when, where, and how fuel is consumed, fleets can identify wasteful behaviors or inefficient routes.

- *Fuel Purchase Strategies*: Data can guide decisions about when and where to purchase fuel, potentially leading to bulk discounts or avoiding high-cost areas.

Future Trends: AI, IoT, and Autonomous Vehicles

As technology evolves, fleet management stands to benefit significantly from innovations on the horizon.

1. **Artificial Intelligence (AI):**

- *Data Analysis*: AI can sift through vast amounts of data faster and more accurately than humans, identifying patterns and offering actionable insights.
- *Driver Assistance Systems*: AI can provide real-time assistance to drivers, suggesting route changes or alerting to potential hazards.

2. **Internet of Things (IoT):**

- *Vehicle-to-Vehicle Communication*: Vehicles can communicate with each other, sharing information about road conditions, traffic, or other relevant data.
- *Remote Diagnostics*: Sensors within the vehicle can relay information to central systems or manufacturers, providing real-time health checks and facilitating remote diagnostics.

3. **Autonomous Vehicles:**

- *Safety Improvements*: By reducing human error, autonomous vehicles have the potential to significantly decrease accidents.
- *Operational Efficiency*: Without the need for driver rest periods, autonomous fleets could operate more continuously, potentially improving efficiency and reducing delivery times.

In conclusion, technology and data analysis play a critical role in modern fleet management. By adopting and integrating these tools, fleet operators can improve safety, efficiency, and cost-effectiveness, positioning themselves for success in an ever-evolving landscape.

Chapter 4: Operations and Logistics

Planning and Scheduling

The backbone of any successful fleet operation lies in meticulous planning and scheduling. This not only maximizes fleet utilization but also minimizes downtime and ensures timely deliveries.

1. **Understanding Demand**:

- *Frequency Analysis*: Determine peak demand times versus off-peak periods.
- *Load Assessment*: Estimate the average size and weight of consignments to determine the appropriate vehicle type.

2. **Scheduling Framework**:

- *Static Scheduling*: Establishing fixed schedules based on routine or predictable demands.
- *Dynamic Scheduling*: Adapting to unexpected demands or real-time adjustments.

3. **Balancing Fleet Utilization**:

- *Rotational Schedules*: Ensure that vehicles are used evenly, preventing overuse of certain units.
- *Scheduled Downtime*: Plan for regular maintenance to reduce unexpected breakdowns.

Route Optimization for Efficiency and Sustainability

Selecting the optimal route is crucial not just for timely deliveries but also for fuel savings and reducing the carbon footprint.

1. **Analytical Tools**:

- *Geospatial Analysis*: Using geographic data to determine the shortest and quickest routes.
- *Traffic Prediction Models*: Analyze historic traffic data to anticipate slowdowns or congestion.

2. **Sustainability Considerations**:

- *Fuel Efficiency*: Choosing routes that reduce fuel consumption by minimizing stops and starts or elevation changes.

- *Eco-routing*: Identifying routes that minimize environmental impact, even if they aren't the shortest or quickest.

3. **Real-time Adjustments**:

- *Live Traffic Feed Integration*: Adjust routes on-the-fly based on live traffic conditions.
- *Weather Predictions*: Avoid routes that may be affected by adverse weather conditions.

Driver Allocation and Management

Arguably, drivers are the most vital assets in fleet management. Properly managing and allocating them can improve efficiency and morale.

1. **Driver Skill Assessment**:

- *Specialization*: Some drivers might be more skilled with certain vehicle types or routes.
- *Training Levels*: Ensure drivers are adequately trained for the tasks assigned, including special cargo handling or safety procedures.

2. **Health and Fatigue Management**:

- *Mandatory Rest Periods*: Ensure drivers take legally mandated breaks.
- *Health Check-ups*: Regular health assessments can prevent potential issues on the road.

3. **Performance Monitoring and Feedback**:

- *Telematics Data*: Monitor driving habits to provide constructive feedback.
- *Reward Programs*: Recognize and reward exceptional performance to motivate and retain drivers.

Crisis and Contingency Management

In the world of fleet management, crises are inevitable, be it due to vehicle breakdowns, accidents, or external factors like natural disasters. Effective crisis and contingency management can mitigate these challenges.

1. **Risk Assessment**:

- *Regular Audits*: Identify potential vulnerabilities in the fleet's operations.

- *External Threat Analysis*: Understand external risks, such as geopolitical events or natural disasters.

2. **Contingency Planning**:

- *Alternative Routes*: Always have backup routes planned.
- *Fleet Backup*: Maintain a percentage of the fleet as a buffer for unexpected demands or vehicle breakdowns.

3. **Emergency Response Protocols**:

- *Accident Protocols*: Clearly outline steps drivers should take post-accident, including securing the scene, notifying authorities, and reporting to the fleet manager.
- *Breakdown Procedures*: Ensure drivers know who to call and what to do in case of vehicle failures, and have access to a network of repair services.

4. **Post-Crisis Analysis**:

- *Debriefing Sessions*: After any significant crisis, conduct a debrief to understand what went wrong and how to prevent it in the future.
- *Continuous Improvement*: Regularly update contingency plans based on new insights and changing scenarios.

Effective operations and logistics management is akin to a well-oiled machine. With meticulous planning, continuous optimization, proactive driver management, and robust crisis handling procedures, fleet managers can ensure smooth and efficient operations, minimizing disruptions and maximizing productivity.

Chapter 5: Maintenance and Upkeep

Importance of Regular Maintenance Checks

Reliable fleet performance is rooted in systematic and regular maintenance checks. These not only extend the lifespan of vehicles but also ensure safety and optimal efficiency.

1. **Safety Considerations**:

- *Accident Prevention*: Regular checks can detect potential issues before they lead to failures or accidents.
- *Regulatory Compliance*: Many regions have strict safety standards, and consistent maintenance helps fleets adhere to these regulations.

2. **Efficiency and Longevity**:

- *Maximizing Asset Lifespan*: Routine maintenance can significantly extend the functional life of vehicles, providing a better return on investment.

- *Fuel Efficiency*: A well-maintained vehicle consumes fuel more efficiently and reduces overall operational costs.

3. **Operational Continuity**:

- *Reduced Downtime*: Detecting and addressing issues early can prevent prolonged vehicle downtimes.
- *Predictability*: A regular maintenance schedule provides a predictable operational flow.

Predictive vs. Reactive Maintenance

Understanding the difference between predictive and reactive maintenance can determine the longevity and efficiency of a fleet.

1. **Reactive Maintenance**:

- *Definition*: Addressing issues as they arise.
- *Implications*: While sometimes necessary, reactive measures can be more costly in the

long run due to unplanned downtimes and potential secondary damages.

2. **Predictive Maintenance**:

- *Definition*: Anticipating and addressing issues before they become significant problems.
- *Benefits*: Reduces unforeseen downtimes, prolongs vehicle life, and often results in cheaper and less extensive repairs.

Role of Technology in Maintenance

Technology has transformed how fleet maintenance is approached, making it more precise, efficient, and predictive.

1. **Telematics**:

- *Real-time Monitoring*: Sensors can immediately detect and report anomalies in vehicle performance.
- *Historical Data Analysis*: By analyzing historical data, patterns of wear and tear can be discerned, facilitating predictive maintenance.

2. **Maintenance Management Software**:

- *Automated Scheduling*: Software can generate and track maintenance schedules, sending reminders when checks or interventions are due.
- *Digital Records*: Electronic logs ensure detailed maintenance histories for each vehicle, aiding in future inspections or resale evaluations.

Cost Optimization Strategies

Effective maintenance doesn't necessarily mean costly maintenance. Several strategies can optimize costs without compromising vehicle health.

1. **Bulk Purchasing**:

- *Parts and Supplies*: Buying replacement parts in bulk or during sales can lead to significant savings.

2. **In-house vs. Outsourced Maintenance**:

- *Assessment*: Consider the costs and benefits of having an in-house maintenance team versus outsourcing to specialized service providers.

3. **Training and Workshops**:

- *Skill Development*: Regularly train in-house teams, ensuring they are up-to-date with the latest maintenance techniques and technologies.

4. **Warranty Utilization**:

- *Warranty Tracking*: Ensure that all warranty-covered repairs or replacements are claimed.

Required Maintenance File Retention

Maintaining accurate and comprehensive maintenance records is not just good practice—it's often a legal necessity.

1. **Components of a Maintenance File**:

- *Service Logs*: Detailed accounts of every service intervention, including date, nature of service, parts replaced, and personnel involved.
- *Inspection Reports*: Results of any safety or regulatory inspections.

- *Warranty Documents*: Documentation pertaining to parts warranties or vehicle warranties.

2. **Benefits of Proper File Retention**:

- *Regulatory Compliance*: Many jurisdictions require fleets to retain maintenance records for specified periods to demonstrate adherence to safety and operational standards.
- *Resale Value*: Comprehensive maintenance records can enhance a vehicle's resale value by providing potential buyers with a full service history.
- *Dispute Resolution*: In case of disagreements with service providers or warranty claims, detailed records provide necessary evidence.

3. **Digital Transformation**:

- *Digital Repositories*: Transition from paper files to digital records for easy retrieval, duplication, and analysis.

- *Cloud Storage*: Utilize cloud storage solutions to ensure data safety and accessibility from any location.

By emphasizing timely maintenance and leveraging technology, fleet managers can ensure vehicle longevity, safety, and operational continuity. Proper record-keeping further solidifies this approach, ensuring compliance, transparency, and future readiness.

Chapter 6: Driver Management and Safety

Hiring and Training the Right Drivers

The success of any fleet management system hinges largely on the drivers at the helm of the vehicles. Ensuring you hire and train the best is paramount.

1. **Recruitment Strategies**:

- *Defining Criteria*: Determine essential qualifications, experience levels, and desired soft skills.
- *Background Checks*: Comprehensive checks including previous employment, driving history, and any criminal records.

2. **Training Programs**:

- *Orientation*: Familiarize new drivers with company culture, fleet operations, and expectations.
- *Skill Enhancement*: Offer advanced driving courses or specialized training for specific vehicle types.
- *Continuous Learning*: Regular refresher courses to keep skills sharp and updated.

Monitoring Driver Behavior and Performance

With the help of technology and systematic reviews, it's possible to ensure drivers are at their best at all times.

1. **Telematics and Real-time Monitoring**:

- *Driving Metrics*: Monitor speed, braking patterns, cornering, and idling to assess driving habits.
- *Feedback Loops*: Use data to provide constructive feedback to drivers.

2. **Performance Reviews**:

- *Periodic Evaluations*: Regularly assess drivers based on performance metrics, feedback from clients, and adherence to schedules.

Promoting Safety Culture and Training

- Safety is a cornerstone of fleet management. Promoting a strong safety culture can prevent accidents, save costs, and protect the company's reputation.

1. **Safety First Orientation**:

- *Induction Programs*: Emphasize the importance of safety from the first day.
- *Safety Champions*: Appoint and recognize drivers who consistently demonstrate exceptional safety standards.

2. **Training Modules**:

- *Simulated Drills*: Use simulators to mimic challenging driving scenarios, training drivers to handle them.
- *Emergency Protocols*: Educate drivers about the steps to follow in emergencies, including accident reporting, first aid, and hazard management.

Legal Requirements and Compliance

Staying abreast of legal requirements is essential not only for the safety of drivers and the public but also to avoid costly penalties or legal battles.

1. **Licensing**:

- *Proper Documentation*: Ensure all drivers possess valid licenses for the vehicles they operate.
- *Renewal Checks*: Monitor and remind drivers of upcoming license renewals.

2. **Regulations**:

- *Local Laws*: Different jurisdictions might have varying rules concerning driving hours, rest periods, and cargo restrictions. Ensure compliance.
- *Periodic Medical Checks*: Many regions mandate regular health checks for commercial drivers.

Driver Qualification (DQ) Files and Requirements

A vital part of compliance is maintaining comprehensive Driver Qualification (DQ) files, which verify a driver's eligibility and qualifications.

Components of a DQ File:

1. **Driver's Application for Employment**

Must be completed in full and signed by the driver.

2. **Inquiry to Previous Employers (3 years)**

Documented inquiries to past employers regarding the driver's safety performance history.

3. **Record of Responses from Previous Employers**

Any records of responses received from previous employers.

4. **Inquiry to State Agencies for Driver's Driving Record**

Obtain a Motor Vehicle Record (MVR) from every state where the driver held a motor vehicle license or permit during the past 3 years.

5. **Annual Review of Driving Record**

An annual review to ensure the driver meets minimum requirements for safe driving.

6. **Driver's Certification of Violations and Annual Review**

Once a year, drivers must provide a list of all convictions for traffic violations in the past 12 months.

7. **Medical Examiner's Certificate**

Indicates that the driver is medically qualified to operate a commercial motor vehicle. Depending on the driver's health, these certificates are valid for up to 2 years.

8. **Road Test Certificate**

Proof that the driver has successfully completed a road test and is capable of operating the kind of commercial motor vehicle he or she will be assigned.

9. **If applicable, a Copy of the Driver's CDL (Commercial Driver's License)**

If the employer uses a copy of the CDL in lieu of a road test certificate for drivers who operate a commercial motor vehicle, that requires a CDL.

10. **Verification of the Driver's Employment History (10 years for drivers operating a vehicle that requires a CDL)**

This might overlap with the inquiry to previous employers but covers a longer period.

11. **Drug and Alcohol Testing Results**

This should include pre-employment drug test results and any subsequent testing records (like random testing results, post-accident test results, etc.).

12. **Training Certificates**

If the driver went through any training, especially any mandatory training as per FMCSA requirements.

13. **Entry-Level Driver Training Certificate**

If applicable, proof that an entry-level driver has completed the required training.

14. **Driver's Statement of On-Duty Hours**

For drivers who are newly hired and have worked for another employer within the previous 7 days. This ensures compliance with federal hours-of-service regulations.

15. Longer Combination Vehicle (LCV) Driver Training Certificate

If applicable, evidence that the driver has been trained in the operation of longer combination vehicles.

16. Skill Performance Evaluation (SPE) Certificate

If applicable, for drivers with a physical impairment who successfully demonstrate the ability to operate a commercial vehicle safely.

Clearinghouse Query Requirement:

1. **Pre-Employment Query**: Before hiring a new driver, employers are required to conduct a full query of the Clearinghouse to ensure that the driver has no unresolved positive drug or alcohol test results or refusals to test from past employers. This is necessary before allowing the driver to perform any safety-sensitive function.

2. **Annual Query**: Employers are also required to query the Clearinghouse at least once a year for every driver they currently employ to confirm

that no violation has occurred in the past year outside of the employer's purview.

3. **Consent Required**: To conduct a full query, employers need the driver's consent. The consent process takes place within the Clearinghouse, and if the driver does not provide consent, they cannot be used for safety-sensitive functions.

4. **Records**: Employers are required to keep records of all queries and information obtained from the Clearinghouse. This can be part of the DQ file.

Proper driver management is multifaceted, ranging from the hiring phase to regular performance monitoring. By prioritizing safety, ensuring legal compliance, and meticulously maintaining DQ files, fleet managers can safeguard their operations, drivers, and the public at large.

Chapter 7: Fuel Management

Strategies for Fuel Efficiency

Managing fuel consumption is both an economic and environmental imperative. By optimizing fuel efficiency, companies can reduce costs and minimize their ecological impact.

1. **Driver Training**:

- *Eco-Driving Techniques*: Train drivers in methods that reduce fuel consumption, such as gentle acceleration and braking, maintaining optimal speeds, and avoiding excessive idling.
- *Regular Feedback*: Provide drivers with feedback on their fuel efficiency to encourage more responsible behavior.

2. **Vehicle Maintenance**:

- *Regular Checks*: Ensure engines are tuned, and filters are clean to optimize fuel consumption.

- *Tire Maintenance*: Regularly check tire pressure and alignment; under-inflated or misaligned tires can increase fuel consumption.

3. **Route Optimization**:

- *Traffic Avoidance*: Use real-time traffic data to avoid congested routes.
- *Route Planning Tools*: Employ advanced tools to find the shortest and most fuel-efficient paths.

Alternative Fuels and Their Relevance

With the global shift towards sustainability, alternative fuels have become an essential consideration for fleet management.

1. **Types of Alternative Fuels**:

- *Electricity*: Electric vehicles (EVs) are increasingly popular due to their low operating costs and zero emissions.
- *Natural Gas*: Compressed Natural Gas (CNG) and Liquefied Natural Gas (LNG) offer lower emissions compared to traditional fuels.

- *Biofuels*: Derived from organic materials, biofuels can be a renewable and less polluting alternative.
- *Hydrogen*: Fuel cell vehicles use hydrogen gas to produce electricity, emitting only water vapor as a byproduct.

2. **Relevance in Fleet Management**:

- *Cost Savings*: Some alternative fuels can be more economical in the long run, considering fuel prices and potential tax incentives.
- *Environmental Responsibility*: Transitioning to cleaner fuels can significantly reduce a fleet's carbon footprint.
- *Regulatory Compliance*: Many regions are introducing stringent emission standards, making a shift to alternative fuels necessary.

Implementing Fuel Card Programs

Fuel card programs can streamline the process of fuel purchasing, offering both convenience and potential savings.

1. **Benefits of Fuel Cards**:

- *Consolidated Billing*: Receive a single, itemized bill for all fleet fuel purchases.
- *Discounts and Rewards*: Many fuel card providers offer discounts or reward programs.
- *Expense Monitoring*: Track and analyze fuel expenses in real-time.

2. **Choosing the Right Program**:

- *Coverage*: Ensure the card is accepted at a wide range of stations, especially if the fleet operates over extensive areas.
- *Security Features*: Opt for cards with security measures like PIN protection or driver ID requirements to prevent unauthorized use.

3. **Integration with Fleet Management Systems**:

- *Data Collection*: Integrate fuel card data with fleet management software to track and analyze fuel consumption per vehicle or driver.
- *Expense Management*: Streamline budgeting and financial forecasting with consolidated fuel expenditure data.

Measuring and Reducing Fleet Carbon Footprint

With increasing awareness about climate change, fleets are under pressure to reduce their carbon footprints.

1. **Assessment**:

- *Emission Tracking Tools*: Use specialized tools to measure the fleet's carbon emissions based on fuel consumption, vehicle types, and distance traveled.
- *Benchmarking*: Compare your fleet's emissions with industry standards or competitors to identify areas for improvement.

2. **Reduction Strategies**:

- *Fleet Modernization*: Gradually replace older vehicles with newer, more fuel-efficient, or low-emission models.

- *Alternative Fuels*: As discussed, transitioning to cleaner fuels can drastically cut emissions.
- *Idle Reduction Programs*: Encourage drivers to turn off engines during prolonged stops.
- *Aerodynamics*: Retrofit vehicles with aerodynamic features like side skirts or roof fairings to reduce wind resistance and improve fuel efficiency.

3. **Offsetting Emissions**:

- *Carbon Offsets*: Invest in carbon offset projects such as reforestation or renewable energy to neutralize a portion of the fleet's emissions.
- *Partner with Green Initiatives*: Collaborate with environmental organizations or initiatives that aim to reduce the global carbon footprint.

Effective fuel management is no longer just about cost-saving—it's a multifaceted discipline that addresses efficiency, sustainability, and the broader responsibility of businesses towards the environment. By adopting advanced strategies and technologies, fleets can lead the charge in crafting a greener, more sustainable future.

Chapter 8: Cost Control and Budgeting

Understanding the Cost Elements of Fleet Management

Before any cost control or budgeting measures can be implemented, it is vital to have a comprehensive understanding of the different costs associated with fleet management.

1. **Fixed Costs**:

- *Vehicle Acquisition*: Whether buying or leasing, the upfront or recurring costs of obtaining vehicles.
- *Licensing and Insurance*: Mandatory fees associated with vehicle operation.
- *Depreciation*: The loss in value of vehicles over time, crucial for fleets that own their vehicles.

2. **Operational Costs**:

- *Fuel*: One of the most significant recurring expenses.
- *Maintenance and Repairs*: Regular upkeep and unexpected repairs.
- *Employee Salaries*: Wages for drivers, technicians, and administrative staff.
- *Telematics and Software*: Costs associated with fleet management software, GPS, and other technological tools.

3. **Incidental Costs**:

- *Fines and Penalties*: From traffic violations or non-compliance with regulations.
- *Accident-related Expenses*: Repairs, medical bills, or insurance claims from accidents.

Setting and Adhering to Budgets

Budgeting is the process of assigning a monetary value to each of the above cost elements, anticipating them, and ensuring they are met without unexpected overruns.

1. **Creating a Comprehensive Budget**:

- *Historical Data*: Analyze past expenditures to forecast future budgets.
- *Involve Stakeholders*: Get input from drivers, maintenance teams, and managers for a holistic budget.

2. **Monitoring**:

- *Regular Reviews*: Monthly or quarterly reviews to compare actual expenditures against the budget.
- *Real-time Monitoring Tools*: Use fleet management software to track real-time expenditures, especially for fuel and maintenance.

3. **Adjustments**:

- *Flexibility*: Have provisions for unexpected expenses. Adjust budgets if consistent overruns in certain categories are observed.

Reducing Operational Costs

- With a clear understanding of the costs, measures can be taken to reduce them without compromising fleet efficiency.

1. **Fuel Efficiency**:

- As discussed in the previous chapter, adopting strategies for fuel management can lead to substantial savings.

2. **Preventative Maintenance**:

- Regularly maintaining vehicles can prevent major, more expensive repairs in the future.

3. **Optimized Routes**:

- Efficient route planning reduces fuel costs and wear and tear on vehicles.

4. **Bulk Purchasing**:

- Procure items like spare parts, tires, and even fuel (if storage is available) in bulk to leverage discounts.

5. **Retraining and Feedback**:

- Continuous driver training and feedback can reduce costs associated with accidents, fuel inefficiency, and vehicle misuse.

Future-proofing Investments

Looking ahead is crucial in fleet management to ensure that investments made today do not become obsolete or burdensome liabilities tomorrow.

1. **Technological Investments**:

    - Invest in adaptable fleet management systems that can be updated as technology progresses.

    - Look for scalable solutions that can grow with the size and needs of the fleet.

2. **Vehicle Purchases**:

    - Prioritize vehicles with a reputation for longevity, low maintenance, and good resale value.

- Consider the potential rise of alternative fuels when buying. For instance, purchasing a diesel truck might not be wise if regulations are phasing out diesel in the near future.

3. **Training**:

   - Regularly update training programs to ensure drivers and staff are prepared for upcoming industry shifts.

4. **Regulatory Awareness**:

   - Stay informed about regulatory changes that could impact fleet operations. This includes emission standards, alternative fuel incentives, and safety regulations.

Cost control and budgeting form the backbone of efficient fleet management. By understanding costs, meticulously planning and monitoring budgets, actively seeking ways to reduce expenses, and preparing for the future, fleet managers can ensure financial stability and sustainability for their operations.

Chapter 9: Compliance and Regulatory Landscape

Overview of Regulatory Bodies

Fleet management doesn't operate in a vacuum. Numerous regulatory bodies govern various aspects of fleet operations, ensuring safety, environmental responsibility, and other societal benefits.

1. **Department of Transportation (DOT):**

   - Oversees the national transportation system.

   - Establishes safety regulations, especially for commercial vehicles.

2. **Environmental Protection Agency (EPA):**

   - Sets and enforces regulations related to vehicle emissions.

   - Plays a significant role in encouraging or mandating the use of alternative fuels.

3. **Local State Agencies**:

  - Different states may have their own specific regulations, especially regarding vehicle registration, roadworthiness, and emission standards.

4. **International Regulatory Bodies**:

  - For fleets operating internationally, various country-specific organizations and agreements might come into play.

Keeping Up with Local and International Regulations

Ensuring continuous compliance requires vigilance and proactive efforts:

1. **Continuous Education**:

  - Attend seminars, workshops, and conferences dedicated to fleet compliance.

  - Subscribe to industry publications and updates.

2. **Networking**:

- Join fleet management associations and forums. Engaging with peers can help you stay updated about common challenges and solutions.

3. **Employ Dedicated Compliance Officers**:

- For larger fleets, having staff members dedicated to compliance can be invaluable.

4. **Leverage Technology**:

- Utilize fleet management software that offers regulatory updates and compliance monitoring features.

Impact of Non-compliance

Ignoring or overlooking regulations can have severe repercussions:

1. **Financial Penalties**:

   - Fines and sanctions can be levied against companies that fail to meet regulatory standards.

2. **Operational Disruptions**:

   - Vehicles may be grounded or impounded if they're found non-compliant, disrupting business operations.

3. **Legal Implications**:

   - In extreme cases, persistent non-compliance could lead to legal actions against the company or its executives.

4. **Reputational Damage**:

   - Public knowledge of non-compliance can harm a company's reputation, leading to lost business opportunities.

Regular Audits and Reviews

Periodic checks are essential to ensure continuous compliance:

1. **Internal Audits**:

   - Regularly review processes, documents, and vehicle conditions to ensure they align with regulatory standards.

2. **Third-party Audits**:

   - Occasionally, getting an external expert to audit your fleet can provide an unbiased view of your compliance status.

3. **Feedback Loop**:

   - After every audit, implement recommended changes and monitor their effectiveness.

DQ (Driver Qualification) Files

Maintaining detailed DQ files is vital for compliance with many DOT regulations.

1. **What's Included**:

   - *Driver's License Information*: Must be updated regularly.

- *Employment Application*: Detailed application specifically for the driving position.

- *Road Test Certification*: Or a copy of the commercial driver's license as an equivalent.

- *Medical Examiner's Certificate*: Proving the driver is medically fit to operate the vehicle.

- *Driver's Record from Previous Employers*: Usually for the past three years.

- *Annual Driving Record Review*: Ensuring the driver continues to meet regulatory requirements.

- *Annual Certificate of Violations*: The driver lists all violations from the past year.

2. **Importance**:

- Ensures that every driver is qualified and capable.

- Provides a centralized repository of driver information, which can be crucial during audits or in case of accidents.

Maintenance Files

Consistent vehicle maintenance is not just about efficiency; it's also a regulatory requirement.

1. **What's Included**:

   - *Maintenance Schedule*: A detailed plan of regular checks and services.

   - *Repair Records*: Detailed accounts of all repairs, parts replaced, and costs involved.

   - *Vehicle Inspection Reports*: Both daily reports from drivers and annual inspection reports.

   - *Warranty Documents and Recall Notices*: To ensure that the vehicle gets all due services and updates.

2. **Importance**:

- Ensures that vehicles remain in safe and operable condition.

- Provides a comprehensive record that can be referenced during regulatory audits or when deciding on vehicle retirement or resale.

Compliance in fleet management is not a mere formality. It's a responsibility to the safety of drivers, other road users, and the environment. With regular audits, meticulous record-keeping, and an ongoing commitment to staying updated, fleets can navigate the regulatory landscape confidently and efficiently.

Chapter 10: Sustainability and Environmental Responsibility

The Rise of Eco-Friendly Fleets

In an era marked by increasing environmental concerns and a push towards sustainable practices, fleet management isn't left behind. The transportation sector, being a significant contributor to global carbon emissions, is under pressure to shift towards eco-friendly practices.

1. **Drivers of Change**:

- *Regulatory Push*: Governments worldwide are setting stringent emission standards and offering incentives for green transitions.
- *Corporate Responsibility*: Companies are recognizing their role in environmental protection and are keen to showcase sustainable operations for branding and ethics.

- *Public Demand*: With a rise in eco-consciousness, customers prefer associating with environmentally responsible companies.

Benefits of Green Fleet Management

- Transitioning to eco-friendly fleets isn't just about environment preservation. It carries tangible benefits:

1. **Cost Savings**:

- Reduced fuel costs, especially with electric or hybrid vehicles.
- Potential for tax credits, rebates, and reduced registration fees for green vehicles.

2. **Improved Corporate Image**:

- A green fleet can be a significant PR and marketing tool, projecting the company as forward-thinking and responsible.

3. **Reduced Carbon Footprint**:

- Directly contributing to global efforts to combat climate change.

4. **Operational Longevity**:

- Electric vehicles often come with fewer moving parts, translating to reduced maintenance needs and longer operational lifespans.

Transitioning to Electric and Hybrid Vehicles

- Making the shift to cleaner technologies is the cornerstone of green fleet management.

1. **Assessment and Planning**:

- Analyze the current fleet's environmental impact.
- dentify routes and vehicles that can be easily transitioned to electric or hybrid models.

2. **Infrastructure Development**:

- Ensure the availability of charging stations, either by leveraging existing infrastructure or by investing in proprietary charging hubs.

3. **Training and Onboarding**:

- Drivers need to be educated about operating electric or hybrid vehicles, including efficient driving practices and charging protocols.

4. **Monitoring and Upgradation**:

- Regularly assess the performance of electric/hybrid vehicles.
- Stay updated with advancements in green vehicle technology and plan phased upgrades.

Case Studies of Successful Green Fleet Transformations

1. City Transport Service, XYZ City:

- Transitioned 50% of their buses to electric models by 2022.
- Achieved a 40% reduction in operational costs and a significant reduction in city pollution levels.
- Used the savings to invest in further expanding the electric bus fleet.

2. ABC Logistics Company:

- Shifted to a hybrid model for their inter-city delivery trucks, resulting in a 30% decrease in fuel consumption.
- Partnered with local communities to set up solar-powered charging stations, further pushing their sustainability agenda.

3. Global Ride-Sharing Giant, RideGreen:

- Introduced incentives for drivers to shift to electric vehicles.
- Collaborated with vehicle manufacturers to get bulk discounts on electric cars for their drivers.
- Within three years, 60% of their fleet in major metropolitan areas became electric.

Embracing sustainability in fleet management is the way forward. With tangible operational and environmental benefits, it's a move that aligns with both business and ethical considerations. The transition might come with challenges, but with careful planning and a commitment to the cause, it is an achievable and worthy goal.

Chapter 11: Crisis Management and Contingency Planning

Importance of Being Prepared

In the unpredictable world of fleet management, emergencies are not just possible—they're probable. From sudden vehicle breakdowns to major accidents or natural disasters affecting transportation routes, a plethora of crises can hit at any time.

1. **Operational Continuity**: A crisis can disrupt operations, leading to delays, missed deliveries, or halted services. Being prepared ensures minimal disruption.

2. **Safety**: The safety of drivers, other staff, and assets becomes paramount during a crisis. Preparedness can save lives and reduce property damage.

3. **Financial Implications**: A well-managed crisis can prevent loss of revenue and potential legal liabilities.

4. **Reputation Management**: A company that manages crises efficiently can retain customer trust and even enhance its reputation.

Identifying Potential Risks and Challenges

To be prepared, you first need to know what you're preparing for. This step involves a deep dive into potential scenarios that might disrupt operations.

1. **Risk Assessment**:

- Engage in regular brainstorming sessions with key stakeholders to identify possible risks.
- Analyze past incidents in the company as well as industry-wide events.

2. **Risk Categorization**:

- Categorize risks based on severity and likelihood. For instance, vehicle breakdowns might be frequent but low-severity, while natural disasters are infrequent but high-severity.

3. **Continuous Monitoring**:

- Implement systems to monitor and detect emerging risks, from traffic jams to political unrest in regions affecting supply routes.

Creating a Comprehensive Crisis Response Plan

With identified risks in hand, the next step is formulating a detailed response for each scenario.

1. **Designate a Crisis Team**:

- Assign roles such as team leader, communicator, and log keeper.
- Ensure this team undergoes regular training and simulation exercises.

2. **Detailed Action Plans**:

- For each identified risk, have a step-by-step action plan.
- Include contact details of all key personnel, emergency services, and backup vendors.

3. **Communication Protocol**:

- Establish clear communication channels, ensuring real-time updates to relevant stakeholders.
- Pre-draft messages or templates for common scenarios to ensure quick and accurate communication.

4. **Resource Allocation**:

- Maintain an emergency reserve of resources such as vehicles, funds, or alternative accommodation for drivers stranded due to crises.

Post-crisis Evaluation and Learning

Every crisis, no matter how well managed, provides an opportunity to learn and refine future responses.

1. **Debriefing Sessions**:

- After the immediate crisis has passed, gather the crisis team and other involved parties for a detailed debrief.

2. **Feedback Collection**:

- Get feedback from all levels—from drivers on the ground to top-level management.

3. **Document Everything**:

- Ensure all actions, challenges, and resolutions during the crisis are documented. This will be invaluable for training and refining future plans.

4. **Refine the Crisis Plan**:

- Based on the learnings, make necessary adjustments to the crisis response plan.

5. **Training and Simulations**:

- Regularly engage the team in simulation exercises, incorporating recent learnings to ensure they're prepared for real-life scenarios.

In conclusion, while no organization wishes to face a crisis, the reality is they are often inevitable. The difference between organizations that weather the storm successfully and those that falter lies in preparation, agility, and an unwavering commitment to safety and operational integrity. Through meticulous planning, regular training, and continuous learning, fleet management can turn crises into opportunities for growth and organizational resilience.

Chapter 12: The Future of Fleet Management

The Impact of Autonomous Vehicles

- Autonomous vehicles (AVs) have progressed from science fiction to imminent reality, promising to revolutionize the fleet management landscape.

1. **Operational Efficiency**:

- Reduced human error means fewer accidents and operational interruptions.
- 24/7 operation without concerns for driver fatigue.

2. **Cost Management**:

- Potential for reduced labor costs.
- Predictable and efficient driving patterns can lead to fuel savings.

3. **Safety Enhancements**:

- Advanced sensors and decision-making algorithms in AVs can drastically reduce accident rates.

4. **Challenges and Considerations**:

- Regulatory hurdles and liabilities associated with autonomous operations.
- Need for infrastructure compatible with AV operation.

Integration of AI and Machine Learning

With an ever-increasing amount of data generated by fleets, AI and machine learning provide tools to harness this information for improved decision-making.

1. **Predictive Maintenance**:

- Algorithms can analyze vehicle data and predict when parts are likely to fail, scheduling maintenance more effectively.

2. **Route Optimization**:

- AI can analyze countless route variables in real-time, ensuring the most efficient path.

3. **Demand Forecasting**:

- Predict future fleet demands based on historical data, seasonality, and market trends.

4. **Driver Behavior Analysis**:

- Machine learning models can analyze driver behavior and provide insights or training recommendations.

Changing Dynamics of Fleet Ownership and Sharing Models

The traditional model of owning every vehicle in a fleet is being challenged by new paradigms.

1. **Fleet-as-a-Service (FaaS)**:

- Companies may not need to own a fleet but can access one as required, similar to cloud computing services.

2. **Shared Fleets**:

- Multiple companies or departments sharing a fleet, optimizing utilization.

3. **Subscription Models**:

- Instead of purchasing, companies might subscribe to a fleet service, offering flexibility to scale up or down as required.

Preparing for the Future: Skills, Technologies, and Strategies

The fleet management industry must evolve to stay relevant and competitive. Here's how they can prepare:

1. **Continuous Learning and Training**:

- Equip teams with knowledge about emerging technologies and practices.

2. **Invest in Technology**:

- Prioritize and allocate budgets to incorporate advanced tech solutions.

3. **Strategic Partnerships**:

- Collaborate with tech providers, regulators, and other stakeholders to stay at the forefront of innovation.

4. **Adopt a Flexible Mindset**:

- Be ready to pivot strategies based on technological advancements and market demands.

5. **Focus on Sustainability**:

- As the world moves towards greener solutions, ensure that fleet operations align with environmental goals.

The future of fleet management is on the brink of transformative changes, driven by technological advancements and changing operational paradigms. Embracing these changes requires foresight, adaptability, and a commitment to continuous learning and evolution. Organizations that proactively navigate these waters will not only survive but thrive in the coming decades.

Conclusion

Reflecting on the Changing Nature of Fleet Management

As we journey through the comprehensive contours of fleet management, one thing becomes abundantly clear: the industry is in the midst of a transformative shift. Historically, fleet management was simply about managing a set of vehicles and ensuring they reached from Point A to Point B. Today, it encompasses a myriad of facets, from harnessing AI and big data to proactively thinking about sustainability and environmental impacts. The integration of cutting-edge technologies, evolving regulatory landscapes, and the heightened emphasis on safety and efficiency has redefined the role and challenges of modern fleet managers.

Encouraging Continuous Learning and Adaptation

The dynamism inherent to the current state of fleet management underscores the need for continuous learning and adaptation. Gone are the days where static practices would suffice for decades. The very essence of fleet management now is its fluidity.

1. **Staying Updated**: Whether it's the latest in autonomous vehicle technology, regulatory changes, or best practices in sustainability, being informed is no longer a luxury but a necessity.

2. **Re-skilling and Training**: For organizations, investing in the regular training of their teams is pivotal. This not only enhances operational efficiency but also fosters a culture of growth and adaptability.

3. **Embracing Change**: Resistance to change is a natural human instinct. However, in the rapidly evolving world of fleet management, adaptability is a virtue. Embracing, rather than resisting new technologies or practices, can be the differentiator between industry leaders and those left behind.

The Road Ahead: A Brighter, Efficient, and Sustainable Future

While challenges are aplenty, the future of fleet management is undeniably promising. The integration of technology promises unprecedented levels of efficiency, reducing costs, and enhancing service delivery. The focus on sustainability not only meets regulatory standards but also addresses corporate social responsibilities, contributing to a greener and more sustainable world.

Moreover, as practices become more refined, enhanced safety measures will drastically reduce accidents and mishaps, ensuring the well-being of drivers and assets alike. The transition to more flexible fleet ownership and sharing models will make the industry more resilient, able to quickly adapt to market fluctuations.

In conclusion, the fleet management industry stands at a crossroad of challenges and opportunities. By harnessing the power of technology, staying informed, and adopting a forward-thinking mindset, the road ahead is paved with potential. It's an exciting journey towards a brighter, more efficient, and sustainable future, and every stakeholder has a pivotal role to play in shaping it.

Appendices

Glossary of Terms

Telematics: The integrated use of telecommunications and informatics, used especially in road transportation to relay real-time information about a vehicle.

- **Components**: Often comprises GPS systems, onboard diagnostics, and data recorders.

- **Application**: Used for tracking, fleet management, navigation, insurance, and more.

Autonomous Vehicles (AVs): Vehicles capable of sensing their environment and operating without human involvement.

- **Levels**: Ranges from Level 0 (No Automation) to Level 5 (Full Automation), with increasing capabilities.

- **Enablers**: Relies on sensors like LIDAR, radars, cameras, and sophisticated machine learning algorithms.

- **Benefits**: Potential to improve road safety, optimize traffic flows, and transform urban environments.

Fleet-as-a-Service (FaaS): A business model where companies access a fleet as required rather than owning it.

- **Advantages**: Flexibility in fleet size, reduced ownership responsibilities, and often more economical.

- **Variations**: Can be tailored to various business needs including short-term rentals, long-term leases, or ad-hoc usage.

- **Industry Impact**: Potentially revolutionizes traditional fleet management by adding flexibility and scalability.

Predictive Maintenance: Maintenance strategy driven by the prediction of the future failure of equipment.

- **Technology**: Utilizes data analytics, IoT sensors, and machine learning to forecast equipment failure.

- **Benefits**: Minimizes downtime, extends equipment life, reduces costs, and improves operational efficiency.

- **Application**: Widely used in industries like manufacturing, aviation, and, of course, fleet management.

Total Cost of Ownership (TCO): A financial estimate that helps consumers and enterprise managers determine direct and indirect costs of a product or system.

- **Components**: Initial purchase price, operational costs, maintenance costs, and potential costs of downtime or failures.

- **Relevance**: Especially important in fleet management to assess the real cost of a vehicle beyond its purchase price.

- **Decision-making**: Helps organizations choose between alternatives based on long-term cost implications.

Fleet Compliance: Refers to the adherence of fleet operations to regulations and standards set by governmental and transportation authorities.

- **Importance**: Ensures safety, reduces legal risks, and often leads to operational efficiency.

- **Components**: Includes driver qualifications, vehicle maintenance standards, emissions standards, and operational best practices.

Route Optimization: The process of determining the most efficient route for a vehicle or set of vehicles, considering variables such as traffic, distance, and delivery windows.

- **Technology**: Often uses advanced algorithms and real-time data.

- **Benefits**: Reduces fuel consumption, improves delivery times, and maximizes the productivity of the fleet.

Telemetry: An automated process where measurements and data are collected at remote points and transmitted to receiving equipment for monitoring.

- **Usage in Fleet**: Commonly used to monitor vehicle health, fuel consumption, and other key metrics.

- **Advantages**: Provides real-time insights, helps in proactive problem-solving, and can be integrated with other fleet management systems.

Duty Cycle: Refers to the operational profile of a vehicle, describing how it's driven and for what purpose. It includes factors like driving conditions, frequency, and load.

- **Relevance**: Influences vehicle maintenance schedules and can impact vehicle choice.

- **Implications**: A vehicle's duty cycle can affect its wear and tear, fuel efficiency, and overall longevity.

List of Regulatory Bodies by Region/Country

United States:

• Federal Motor Carrier Safety Administration (FMCSA):

- **Website**: www.fmcsa.dot.gov

- **Role**: An agency within the U.S. Department of Transportation that regulates the trucking industry in the United States. Its primary mission is to prevent commercial motor vehicle-related fatalities and injuries.

- **Main Responsibilities**: Enforcing safety regulations, licensing, and ensuring the fitness of the nation's commercial drivers.

• National Highway Traffic Safety Administration (NHTSA):

- **Website**: www.nhtsa.gov

- **Role**: Responsible for ensuring the safety of motor vehicles and road users in the U.S.

- **Main Responsibilities**: Setting and enforcing vehicle performance standards and regulations, and administering vehicle recall initiatives.

Europe:

- **European Union Road Federation (ERF)**:

  - **Website**: www.erf.be

  - **Role**: A non-profit association representing road infrastructure sector at the European level.

  - **Main Responsibilities**: Advocating for the continuous improvement of road infrastructure and promoting the efficient and sustainable use of roads.

- **European Transport Safety Council (ETSC)**:

  - **Website**: www.etsc.eu

  - **Role**: An independent non-profit organization dedicated to reducing the numbers of deaths and injuries in transport across Europe.

- **Main Responsibilities**: Providing impartial advice and information on transport safety matters to the European Commission, the European Parliament, and EU Member States.

Asia:

• **Asian Association of Road Transport and Infrastructure (AARTI)**:

- **Website**: www.aarti.asia
- **Role**: A collective of Asian nations working together to promote efficient road transport and infrastructure.
- **Main Responsibilities**: Promoting the development of road transport and infrastructure, conducting research, and fostering collaborations between member nations.

Africa:

• **African Transport Policy Program (SSATP)**:

- **Website**: www.ssatp.org

- **Role**: An international partnership to facilitate policy development and related capacity-building in the transport sector in Africa.

- **Main Responsibilities**: Facilitating transport policy dialogue, knowledge generation, and sharing of best practices across the continent.

- **African Roads and Transport Forum (ARTF)**:

  - **Role**: An umbrella organization representing various transport stakeholders in Africa.

  - **Main Responsibilities**: Encouraging cooperation among African nations, promoting sustainable transport initiatives, and ensuring road safety standards are met.

Oceania:

- **National Road Transport Association (NatRoad),** Australia:

  - **Website**: www.natroad.com.au

- **Role**: Represents road freight operators in Australia.

- **Main Responsibilities**: Provides advice on compliance, represents its members at all levels of government, and offers various support services to the road transport industry.

- **NZ Transport Agency**, New Zealand:

  - **Website**: www.nzta.govt.nz

  - **Role**: Oversees land transport safety and infrastructure in New Zealand.

  - **Main Responsibilities**: Licensing, road user safety, and managing the state highway network.

Useful Resources and Further Reading

Online Resources:

Fleet News: A leading source for the latest news in fleet management.

- **Website**: www.fleetnews.co.uk

Fleet Owner: Articles and insights about fleet operations, vehicle technology, and industry data.

- **Website**: www.fleetowner.com

Overdrive: A premier publication for professional drivers and truckers, offering insights on operations, equipment, and regulations.

- **Website**: www.overdriveonline.com

Truckinginfo: Comprehensive news source about trucking and freight transportation.

- **Website**: www.truckinginfo.com

Telematics Providers:

Geotab: Offers a fleet management platform known for its advanced analytics, real-time tracking, and benchmarking capabilities.

- **Website**: www.geotab.com

Samsara: Provides an IoT solution combining hardware, software, and cloud to bring real-time visibility, analytics, and AI to fleet operations.

- **Website**: www.samsara.com

Teletrac Navman: Offers GPS fleet tracking software to assist businesses to manage their vehicles and enhance driver safety.

- **Website**: www.teletracnavman.com

Verizon Connect: Integrates fleet tracking, management, and diagnostic data into one platform to help optimize fleet operations.

- **Website**: www.verizonconnect.com

Mix Telematics: Provides fleet management, driver safety, and vehicle tracking solutions suitable for small and large fleets.

- **Website**: www.mixtelematics.com

JJ Keller: Renowned for their compliance solutions, JJ Keller provides a variety of products and services for fleet management, including telematics and ELD solutions.

- **Website**: www.jjkeller.com